Daughter Raised by Grandmom

Evolved from Emotional Trauma

DELIA L. ADAMS

BALBOA.
PRESS
A DIVISION OF HAY HOUSE

Balboa Press books may be ordered through booksellers or by contacting:

Balboa Press
A Division of Hay House
1663 Liberty Drive
Bloomington, IN 47403
www.balboapress.com
1 (877) 407-4847

Because of the dynamic nature of the Internet, any web addresses or links contained in this book may have changed since publication and may no longer be valid. The views expressed in this work are solely those of the author and do not necessarily reflect the views of the publisher, and the publisher hereby disclaims any responsibility for them.

The author of this book does not dispense medical advice or prescribe the use of any technique as a form of treatment for physical, emotional, or medical problems without the advice of a physician, either directly or indirectly. The intent of the author is only to offer information of a general nature to help you in your quest for emotional and spiritual well-being. In the event you use any of the information in this book for yourself, which is your constitutional right, the author and the publisher assume no responsibility for your actions.

Any people depicted in stock imagery provided by Thinkstock are models, and such images are being used for illustrative purposes only. Certain stock imagery © Thinkstock.

Print information available on the last page.

ISBN: 978-1-5043-9476-5 (sc)
ISBN: 978-1-5043-9478-9 (hc)
ISBN: 978-1-5043-9477-2 (e)

Library of Congress Control Number: 2017919659

Balboa Press rev. date: 01/02/2018

Introduction

At the end of my exhausted self of attempting to make things happen for myself resulted in epic failure due to the emotional trauma I endured throughout my life's paths and journey that disabled me to trust anyone outside myself.

This developed mind set of mine was rooted from the seeds of rejection and abandonment that were planted in me from the womb and catapulted by repeated let downs and disappointments.

Eventually, hopelessness and instability became my navigator. My entire life's aim was consumed with convincing others to love, accept, approve, value and acknowledge my self worth, somehow I thought that would prove that they wanted to be in my life as much as I wanted them in mine.

This desperation and yearning nulled, pulled, antagonized, paralyzed, tormented and robbed me of my true identity and peace of mind.

Fickle was my middle name and self defense was my game. Dysfunction hi jacked my life before I knew my own name. I was born under unfavorable circumstances my parents were both 17 years young.

my biological mother made a decision to give me away to my paternal grandmother to raise me from birth, she resided just one block away in the same household with her parents and birthed three additional children who lived with her.

When I turned three years old my father got married and he and his wife had four more children together. Being the first and only born child between my parents yet, raised by my father's mother coming up in the same household as my aunts and uncles who were more like my older siblings, caused me to begin dealing with a lack of belonging early on.

Displacement and not fitting in was my normal, at some point I began calling my grandmother "mom" right away my aunts quickly remined me that my grand mom wasn't my Mother, although my grand mom was always right there to my defense the truth still hurt.

The times I stayed with my mom I always felt angry within because she never took the initiative to express how much I meant to her. This behavior triggered my thoughts and reminded me that she gave me away because she didn't want me from the start and basically was just tolerating my presence.

As far as my dad was concerned I grew up afraid of him because he wasn't affectionate towards me and was very forward and stern, therefore, I never had that fuzzy feeling of beings daddy's little girl or pretty little princess. My dad demanded to be referred to by his first name. he was present to provide for me financially and to enforce correction never unconditional love expressed directly towards me.

Honestly, whether I was at my mom's house or my dad's I always felt like the throwback kid, highlighted as the visitor and never loved on the same level and affirmation scale as my siblings on both ends of the spectrum at least from my perspective there was always a sense of a split feeling I carried deep within.

Mishap, mistake, unplanned, unwanted, hiccup in life's turn of events were key words that would constantly swarm around in my head. I often wondered was I just the result of two teenagers sneaking to have sex and evidently not a love child.

My realities in life left me vulnerable and on a path called deception looking for love and acceptance in all the wrong places and often times from the wrong people.

This is where God's relentless love meant me with truth and healing in his presence that renewed my mind, transformed my heart and created a right spirit on the inside of me. He lavished me with his caring touch and amplified my hearing of his voice as he satisfied me with living water that began to flow like a well out of my belly and continuously keeps me satisfied to the full and overflow onto the lives of countless others that supersede gender, origin, race, creed or customs. God changed my name from hopeless to hope dealer whereas he's my supplier and Source.

Truth triumphed over my facts of life, my final cry to God for help was a solid and authentic yes! and in that moment of completely letting go of all I thought I knew about him and became like clay willingly to allow him free range without resistance to make me what he planned for me to be in him. God himself instantaneously restored, confirmed, strengthened and established me.

He alone miraculously broke and destroyed the yoke of bondage that plagued my life for many years. During our one on one walk through my transformation and development God began to speak clearly to me about my identity in him before he knitted me in my mother's womb.

It was in this moment that the enemy lost his stronghold and grip off of my life that had caused me to live an unstable lifestyle. God opened up my understanding to the truth of my existence before I came to the earth and that I was born with a purpose, assignment and destiny in him.

He began to help me understand that his plans for my life were decided before I entered the earth realm. He said I formed, designed and predestinated the day I would extract you from your mother's womb in which you refer to as your birthday. Your mother was the vessel I utilized to transport you to the earth.

You belong to me first and my plans for your life have always out ranked the hand you were dealt throughout your life's experience and my thoughts towards you were always higher than if you were unplanned by your earthy parents.

Daughter you were written in my book of life before the foundation of the world. You were birthed into the earth full of purpose for my glory with an assignment attached in your spirit upon your arrival. Although Satan desired to have you and I allowed some of his tactics to buffer you until you were broken enough for your breakthrough.

I prayed for you and kept a hedge of protection around you as you were made ready for my divine use, no man was able to pluck you out of my hand. My handprint was upon you like a birthmark, I never left you alone and I never will. I knew what I had invested on the inside of you.

He began to explain to me that my sins were my symptoms but, not his signature wherefore, the mandate I placed upon your life is this, when you return to your rightful place and are converted strengthen your fellowman. The anointing that I placed upon your life in Jesus name caused your heart to turn back to me continually and reminded you of my relentless and endless love I have towards you in spite of your lack of understanding of who I was as your heavenly father.

These profound truths that God himself downloaded and revealed to me saved my life and my sanity, His relentless love brought me to repentance and gave me the will to live life to the fullest in him. No longer did my circumstances and memories dominate my life's decisions those chains broke off of my emotions. This development process empowered me with the ability to finally be set free from the mental prison that had consumed my thoughts since childhood.

Forgiveness towards everybody I thought treated me poorly, mishandled me or did me wrong on any level became my portion beginning with my loved ones.

Clarity of God's deity and the fact that he is a real God in real time hit my spirit like a lighten bolt that transformed and altered my life entirely. Today I live completely victoriously through staying connected and moving in obedience on demand as I praise God for answering me when I called, the Joy of the Lord is my daily Strength.

For those who have an ear to hear, believe me you God knows the plans he has for you, totally trust him with your whole life and he will lead you into all truth, peace, hope, Joy and an expected end.

An Intimate Relationship with God Is The Master Key That Will Unlock Your Purpose Assignment and Destiny. Perfect Love Cast Out Fear.

1 John 4:18

Dedication

I dedicate this masterpiece to a little darling that I will refer to as special Kay, who God strategically placed in my life that ultimately inspired me to write this book and stirred up the passion on the inside of me to help other little ones around the world as well as speaking to the hurt and unhealed little girl still living on the inside of fully grown woman.

I assure you princess and queen alike that you were fearfully and wonderfully made for the glory of God, daughter of destiny born with divine purpose.

God's will for you is to live your life of abundance and goodness in the land of the living.

Special Kay became a mirror to me in which I saw a clear reflection of myself when I was her age she opened me up to acknowledge and deal with my true buried feelings and unresolved issues and wounds that grew along with me. for my entire life I did not admit or address the affects my circumstances had on me and my unhealthy emotional state and development because, the hurt and pain attached to the memories were heavy hitters, hard to talk about and easier to deny.

Emotional trauma placed a complex upon every area and functions of my life on every level this stigma caused me to develop feelings and thoughts of never being good enough that catapulted to dealing with self hate caused by a lack of assured love and acceptance I desperately desired from both of my parents because I never believed I was made out of love.

Thanks be to God whose UNFAILING love rescued me and desires to rescue you too!!!

And we know that for those who love God all things work together for good, for those who are called according to his purpose.

Romans 8:28

Keynotes

I was a daughter who never bonded with her biological mother caused by her decision to give me away to my paternal Grandmother at birth, seeds of rejection and abandonment were planted in me from the womb and took root that eventually affected every area of my life that developed a defense mechanism that prevented me from trusting others.

I desperately wanted the love, nurturing and special bond with my biological mother that I naturally shared and cherished with my grandmother who raised me, dysfunction hi jacked my life before I knew my own name by the time I was nine years of age silent frustrations developed into emotional trauma.

Life's experiences does not gauge your self worth you were fearfully and wonderfully made daughter of destiny, born into the world to make a unique and invaluable difference.

Seeds Planted In The Womb

In hindsight I could only imagine my young teenage mother who was faced with fear, shame and anxiety having to make a life altering decision for herself and her first unborn baby conceived under unfavorable circumstances. As I rapidly grew on the inside of her I could almost hear her deep thoughts of what have she gotten herself into, so young, scared and simply not ready and totally unprepared to bring another human being into the world to nurture, provide and care for.

I truly believe she made the best decision she could make at the time without a clue of how deeply it would affect the both of us long term. God compensated me with the absolute best grandmother in the world who was my everything she raised me very well with unconditional love, kindness, values, manners, rules, chores and respect as she nurtured me to the best of her ability.

Yet the adoption syndrome created issues along my life's journey. Growing up feeling unloved by the person who gave birth to me didn't leave much room for others to be trusted an inch they didn't stand much of a chance at all. Fear gripped me and kept me from fully opening up to others including GOD scared to death of getting my feelings hurt and being disappointed repeatedly.

By the age of nine I felt completely abandoned and unwanted as a child. Feelings of sadness, and sensitivity took over I would often cry and didn't know how to convey what I was feeling or going through so when I was asked why are you crying? I would say I don't know or not open my mouth to answer at all.

emotional trauma caused me to build walls up and shut all the way down in complete silence until the frustration of whatever turn of event was at hand wore off.

My grandmother was the only person I loved totally with my whole heart because she not only told me she loved me she constantly showed me with her actions.

Unfortunately, I never developed a healthy bond with my mom who passed away in 2013 may she forever rest in peace although we never had this conversation I want you to know I have fully forgiven my mother in my heart as God is my witness who helped me overcome this hard thing over time, He deserve all the GLORY because, at one time I didn't believe I would ever get over the brokenness this reality caused me.

Let's be clear that no matter what the challenges I experienced concerning my mom I still loved her dearly. I just hope I can inspire someone else to evolve from their own personal emotional trauma as well.

Child Play

hild play became discovery time for me especially because I gravitated to older friends, looking back I believe it was because I was brought up around older people being the youngest at the time.

However, during this stage I was introduced to girl on girl grinding which became addictive and opened the door to masturbation as well. Because the others were three to four years older than myself I still considered us all children and didn't understand that I was experiencing molestation. I just knew this feeling felt much better than the hurt and pain I carried around regularly, it gave me a way to escape from the mental torment and sadness I often entertained majority of my time.

This was yet another big secret I kept hidden behind closed doors and never discussed, nor did I really take it all that serious but, little did I know that lesbian spirit would lay dormant and resurface yet again in secret during my adulthood for a long time before coming out eventually in a full blown relationship with another individual years later.

There's a old saying that most people are familiar with that states: what you do in the dark will eventually come to the light.

Let me digress here a moment as early as the age of 5 years old I would sense a pull towards God whom no one formally told me about from time to time, the experience were almost like I would get caught up in a day dream and during that time I would engage into a conversation with God, asking questions like where did I come from? Why am I here on the earth? What is the purpose of people and animals? Where do we all go after we leave the earth?

I knew God was there because it was during these times that I would encounter a outer body experience, but I was too ashamed to share what was happening to me from time to time, I wasn't willing to risk being judged or looked at as strange or crazy on top of all my adoption complexes.

Church

M y family members were not frequent church goers at all, Church attendance wasn't never mandatory for me however I desired to go anyway I was oblivious about the ways of GOD but I fell in love with Church.

Some of my friends didn't have an option about going to church and I always loved going along with a few of them every chance I got.

At 13, I began attending a girl talk session hosted by evangelist sister Witherspoon one of the sweetest woman of God you could ever meet. Although my dad was a Muslim he gave brother and sister Witherspoon permission to transport my sister and I one Saturday of each month to girl talk sessions and they were faithful in getting us there and returning us home. These talks amazed me that every day issues and challenges that people dealt with were found in the word of God.

I remember thinking to myself wow!!! People in the bible went through the same things people today are going through.

These girl talk sessions planted good seeds into my spirit and much fruit came forth from theses enlighten sessions,

I've since created the 411 Hot Topics for the youth and Treasure chest Talks for adults. I developed a passion to inspire and encourage others they way I was influenced and uplifted by the answers in the word of God.

Eventually, I began attending this same church weekly Sunday service as well and became very involved with the works of the church because it gave me a great sense of belonging which made me feel validated and with purpose for my life. A new found place of acceptance had emerged in that moment and it gave me a sense of peace of mind although I began fostering relationships with my new church family the development of my relationship with JESUS was non existent.

Notice I began doing works to be validated, but haven't mentioned having a personal relationship with Jesus. I totally missed understood Jesus purpose and deity for a long time As time went on and I began fostering relationships with some of the church members I began to struggle with balancing my church life with my family life this became overbearing for me at times like playing tug a war. Fearful of fully embracing my spirituality that had a invisible underline of distrust. I was honestly too emotionally damage to walk by faith although I wanted to believe in GOD without a shadow of doubt but it was a great struggle for me.

My family didn't want to hear my church talk as a matter of fact one of my cousins warned me to leave those church folk completely alone he said them people will make you go crazy. not fully understanding God I wasn't willing to give up all I was familiar with out of fear to trust in something I hadn't fully grasped.

However, I was still being drawn although I was feeling wishy washy somehow I knew God loved me and I went to a Wednesday night prayer and bible study in the summertime of 1985

During this service I had a life shaking and undeniable encounter with the living God at 15 years old that left an impression that I was never able to shake even during all my many years of perpetual back sliding.

This encounter happened to me suddenly and powerfully I'm speaking of the baptism of the holy spirit from on high.

I was sitting alone praying and the power of God fell down on me and knocked me to the floor without anyone laying hands on me and I began speaking in a heavenly language as a river a tears flowed down my face uncontrollably as that presence hoovered over me that I remembered as a younger child but this time it was with greater force and power. When I came to myself I was sitting Indian style on the floor of Little David Baptist Church with Mother Anne Thompson by my side praising God and interpreting a message to me from God and what stood out most to me was her repeatedly saying Dee Dee God says you are Special to him and He is going to use you mightily for his service, God has his hand on your life.

The saddest part at the time of this encounter I couldn't fully receive this truth from her or God because I didn't feel or believe I was special. Life's experience can blur your vision and prevent you from seeing yourself as God sees you.

I'm so thankful today that I know we truly are Special to God without a shadow of doubt he created each and everyone of us for fellowship with himself in a unique and special way.

After completing my new members class I shortly got baptized after joining the church and started a more consecrated journey with God. I was so excited that my maternal grandmother was coming to support my new found path and during the baptismal my grandmother stood up to receive Jesus Christ as her personal savior this was a day of double blessings for me.

Now this was my mom's mother whom I loved dearly, grand mom Othelia was as real as they come who spoke her mind and didn't take no mess off of no one.

I can remember like it was yesterday when the invitation of salvation was offered during the service and my Grandmother stood up and stated I believe in Jesus but, I'm not sure if I died right now I would be ready for him to receive me as his own and the preacher responded by telling my grandmother that he appreciated her honesty and lead her in the prayer of salvation.

My grandmother Othelia would give you her last and made sure you would always eat real good her southern roots were from Charlotte North Carolina.

I had a few good years of dedication and commitment until I hit 17 years old sound familiar right? The same age my parents were when I was born, and at 17 a very close family member fondled me in my sleep while attending a family reunion out of state I began to believe the number 17 was cursed over my life but, you will see how God in his Sovereignty turn that curse around into a blessing as only he could do.

My First Love

I won't even hold you I fell head over hills for my first real love. I thought he was the best thing that could happen for me he out ranked any and everything, he mattered most to the point I put him over my own needs and wants.

Eventually I began drifting farther and farther away from my church family and activities.

This was a feeling I had never experienced before and it pulled me all the way into having sex, partying, drinking a little here and there, puffing on joints and on a few occasions popping pills, my mind began to signal to me see all the fun you've been missing out on? Wasting time with them church people. I can remember thinking maybe this Jesus is just a character in the bible story because I still easily went out and resumed my life like I did before receiving him as my personal savior.

What I didn't realize was that God gave us all a free will to chose life or death as well as good or bad and I was simply out of sync with the spirit of God by my own choice.

You're still young would be my thoughts of justification you need to enjoy yourself and have some fun.

You have your whole life to be serious with all that church stuff.

I began to agree with the enemy and allowed his lies to deceive me, I needed to fit in with my peers and feel apart of their circle trying to repair my hurts in attempt to do things on my own.

Reconnecting with my cousins and old friends and making up for lost times became my focus in between every chance I got to spend with my first love.

Little did I know that this was just the beginning of my spiritual yoke of bondage of in and out, up and down, slip and slide and straddling the fence.

This was the very beginning of 32 years of being double minded, patterns and cycles the enemy tried to use to steal my sanity and to abort my purpose in the earth who was born as a daughter of destiny unbeknown to me at that time.

I fell madly in love with Ronald Morgan Bailey who has since passed away, I mention him in loving memory forever and always…. Long as I live you will always be my first Love.

Growing Up

1 988 was the year I graduated from south Philadelphia H.S. which was sort of a prove to my father thing who said I wouldn't graduate so I was determined to make sure I accomplished my goal to prove to myself that I could Do It!!! count that as one black eye for the devil.

However, I was very grateful to God for allowing me to complete H.S. which was an accomplishment that broke the glass ceiling based on going farther than my parents had gone.

Conviction began to play a big part by this time so I returned back to church more gradually and regularly, it's amazing how I viewed God as Church back then but that's what it was at that time of my journey. I equated church attendance with having a relationship with GOD.

This time I signed up to attend main bible school with a few other church members in which I enjoyed immensely during the duration I went I did very well but, I didn't complete the course I bailed out.

I began working my first real job at 12th and chestnut St. in the center city area of Philadelphia as a dental assistant for Dr. Wu's dental office, God gave me favor with Dr. Wu he taught and trained me fully in the dental field himself from taking and reading x rays, making impressions for dentures, sterilizing and setting up instruments to third party billing and file coding as well as assisting him during patient care and procedures.

Within a year I moved with the practice to china town at 9th and Cherry St. as the only African American staff member and was promoted to office manager. Dr. Wu loved when his patients would express to him that they wanted teeth like mine.

This promoted him to do a lot of maintenance work on my teeth for free in which I greatly benefited from for years to come. I'm presently still crazy about my teeth.

I loved everything about my Job and had a special co worker named Anna who was simply awesome.

Dr. Wu enrolled me into a scholarship program that he was affiliated with and I was accepted to attend Still man college in Alabama In sync of finding out I was pregnant at 19 years old.

I chose not to accept the four year college education and decided to focus on taking care of myself and to protect my unborn baby with my life never wanting to pass on that spirit of rejection that had tormented my life.

Thinking back unconsciously I operated in fear which was rooted in distrust the only way I knew to protect myself was to take care of myself without depending on others.

I gave birth to my daughter Brandy who came at 8 months and weighed only 5lbs. 3ozs. January of 1990 three months before my 20th birthday.

If you all could ask my sisters they would tell you how I kept a close watch over my baby and didn't let her come out of my bedroom from January to June because, I trusted no one with my baby and I never wanted her to feel unwanted the way I felt coming up.

Moving Day

I didn't really think my living arrangements all the way through I just wanted to move forward into a better environment for my baby and I.

although I preferred to be married I settled with shacking and moving into his home that didn't belong to me.

Many alone times I would ask myself what has happened with my life? How did I get here? Although I was in my early twenties when I had my baby she became my entire life I was a loner and home body but, it was an intentional decision I made to keep her safe, comfortable, feeling wanted and loved at all times at any cost.

He provided for the household and came and went as he pleased was on his own terms. I often felt stuck between a rock and a hard place.

I stayed to try to create a family that I never had. I wanted my daughter to live and feel loved by both of her parents.

Unhappy, I took up an opportunity to meet up with my first love whom I hadn't seen for a very long time and was very happy to hear from, he wanted to see me and I wanted to see him.

Just like old times he knew the right words I so needed to hear in that moment that made me feel validated and wanted.

The attention by him was music to my ears and I loved feeling missed and special again.

To get right to the point we hooked up sexually that one evening for the last and final time six months later I received a phone call stating that he was killed. I was shock and devastated although we were no longer a couple I never stopped loving him. Fear gripped my heart like a heart attack and I decided to be silence about my present dilemma a secret that I only voiced to God.

Baby Number Two

At Twenty two years old I gave birth to my second baby who was born on schedule at 9 months June of 1992 weighing 7lbs. 14ozs.

Just like that I was a mother of two daughters I remember being in a state of disbelief that I went from no children to having two in a matter of two short years apart.

Life for me in this season was so very unclear and I began to not only feel trapped but paralyzed.

In less than a year I packed up me and my girls and moved in with my grandmother who raised me but, this time she gave me a deadline of 1 year to figure it all out as a mother for me and my children and she held me accountable.

It was time for me to soar on my own and be responsible for me and now my children.

At the time I thought my grandmother was turning on me like everyone else but, she was teaching me how to fight, be strong and survive in this real world standing on my own two feet. It was the best lesson I learned to date.

God bless the child that trust him for their own. At this point of my life it was clear that all of my decisions were being made out of brokenness.

Between, moving into my first very own apartment to working two jobs while taking care of my two girls, and taking on the responsibility of caring for my youngest sister and little cousin I was between sane and crazy by the time I was 24.

My walk with God continue to be as unstable as a rollercoaster ride. For years to come I would be in and out of church in a vicious cycle of patterns that I just couldn't seem to stabilize.

I was going through life winging it as I went along my way. that's the simplest way to put it to say the least.

It was evident at this point of my journey that generational curses had plagued my world on many unhealthy relational levels so yeah any hope I had as a child just seem to get darker and darkner as the years went on.

I feel a strong need to pause right here a moment to stress that although, the enemy is very deceptive and crafty at keeping you distracted and off course with God's purpose while presenting You with custom made trickery that are ultimately later realized to have been counterfeits although, he is strong he's not all knowing therefore, he's consistent at blocking you from getting your breakthrough into light out of dark ness that leads you to your assignment, purpose and ultimate destiny.

Satan knows how to send you a opportunist when you're looking for companionship, a secret enemy in a form of a caring friend, money from someone who keeps you indebted to them and attached to being mishandled for the rest of your natural born life but, I'm here to stress to you that the devil was a liar from the beginning and will lie until the end because he is a certified liar. I'm sure you get the full concept of what I'm conveying Don't fall for his deceiving lies.

You were born for the greater not grave defeat.

Be sober minded; be watchful. Your adversary the devil prowls around like a roaring lion, seeking someone to devour. 1Peter 5:8

Prime example of a counterfeit the key word in that above scripture verse is "like" a fake and or a copy not the real deal nor the original.

KING JESUS is the only Lion from the tribe of Judah and He alone is LORD!!!

Husband

Surely, God has sent me the answer to my prayers and tears, this must be his way of rewarding me for all my hardships and pain that I've endured thus far so I thought finally, someone to help lighten my heavy load and love me unconditionally.

1995, I meant the man of my dreams tall, handsome, respectful and family orientated. We had more things in common than not could this be the one I've been waiting for to give me a moment to exhale and the ability to catch my breathe a moment after being the caregiving to everyone else, finally my chance to breath again be cared for and protected by not just a boyfriend but my husband.

My knight in shining armor had arrived and we went forward full force in a whirl wind of love bliss. once my grandmother gave him a thumbs up he was a keeper for sure in my book.

One year later we had a beautiful wedding and reception with our children, family and friends I had married the man of my dreams November of 1996.

Head over heels I went into protection mode of my newly blended family and retrieved back to church searching for guidance to maintain my new found family unit as one.

I was grateful to God for another chance at building a happy home and family life.

What I didn't know was that my husband wasn't ready for my sudden shift, that had became my normal behavior down through the years.

He felled in love with the not so much church girl. He had no idea how necessary it was for me to seek the face of God on our behalf and not be left to my self will.

My load was heavy taking in 8 to 10 additional family members into our home at one time was overwhelming.

Looking back I wanted to keep their approval of me as the oldest sister they could count on, it took me many years to realize it was only another trap the enemy used to keep me hindered muzzled and bound with oppression that fueled my stagnation.

Then the call that dropped the atomic bomb happened and literally blew me me and my emotions away to no return, my vision of my happy family life crumbled right before my eyes and the scene went pitch black all at once.

Married at 26 and divorced by 33 this wasn't what I vowed or signed up for.

By this point I've come to realize that the collaboration of secrets, infidelities, and poor decision making were all direct results to the dysfunction of my beginnings.

After trying over and over to forgive it actually got harder to do, I couldn't achieve the goal I had set out to reach.

My heart turned ice cold towards the idea of real Love ever being capable of being Real.

I was in such a dark depressed state until I began to agree with my hurt and embraced the idea of not caring anymore,

I developed a it's whatever attitude and I didn't care who liked it or not. I didn't want to care about nobody's feelings especially because I was fully convinced that my feelings didn't matter to no one either.

I constantly convinced myself that Love can't be trusted and it don't last period, point, blank. I have arrived with all my emotional baggage on the road called HOPELESS and I saw no exit once I began walking it's path.

A strong desire for a woman's soft, gentle and caring touch came back upon me strong with a vengeance. I tried to shake it off and then I would dream about encounters and entertaining these thoughts are not a joke.

Spirits are Real people, it's not just a illusion. The enemy knows how to bring you a tailor made desire and make you believe it's a blessing from God. because he knows he has to fully convince you with the very thing he will eventually use to lead to self destruction.

During my break up I entered a same sex relationship with someone I knew a lifetime. Ironically in the past I never was attracted to this individual but I had became very attractive to her at that time and vice versa.

my previous same sex encounters in the past were done in secret and I never considered myself a full blown lesbian because I loved being with men as well.

I must admit that her outward boldness to live out loud motivated me to accept my lifestyle choice out loud as well.

she became very supportive to me both emotionally and financially and I needed both to put my worries to rest.

I felt indebted to her loyalty and this bond developed into a full blown live in relationship quickly.

I want to point out how every poor decision I made was done out of being anxious and never prayerful like the word of God instructs us to do.

It was such a sudden take over until it not only rocked the foundation of my own comfortability but my whole family thought I had a nervous breakdown and was in total disbelief over my decision making.

It was the talk of the entire community that's how much of a shift it was in my lifestyle. Not Minister Delia Adams who hold bible study and Christian fellowships in her home regularly as well as street evangelizing.

everyone attached to me was affected by my life altering decision. I had given the devil full range to use my life as a mockery and to dishonor the God I desperately desired to have a healthy and stable relationship with but didn't know the yoke of bondage that kept me bound was rooted in distrust and fear.

It was out there and I just went with it, this union lasted 9 years and included a commitment service with spoken vows held before family, friends and spectators.

During that time conviction would come and go so I tried to suffice my spiritual need and justify my lifestyle by attending a liberal church, that was led by a gay pastor who was also married to another man although, I was in the lifestyle myself I knew it wasn't what God had designed or planned for marriage.

As challenging as my relationship became the more uneasy things began to get and depression was dominating me. the fun and excitement of going out to the girl clubs with other couples began to wear off I found myself a few times praying to God that the rapture wouldn't take place while I was in there sitting at the bar trying to mask my emptiness I felt on the inside.

Once I began to feel completely uncomfortable about my lifestyle I knew somebody was praying for me because I started sensing my strength returning and my faith building.

At one time I thought God had turned me over to a reprobate mind because of my perpetual backsliding and disobedience.

I thought for sure that God was sick of my faulty behavior because I was sick of myself and didn't know how to get out of it as bad as I wanted to.

At this time I was working second shift at the hospital so when I would get in the shower I began to just talk out loud to God and tell him how sorry I was for constantly letting him down and going my own way without looking to him for guidance, instructions and not totally trusting him about the things that concerned me.

I did this every day in the shower little by little before, I got bolder and bolder and the holy spirit began to bring scriptures back to my remembrance and I would confess them out loud.

One day I began to confess to God that I needed him to perform a miracle on my behalf and after a while I just knew God was going to ANSWER my prayers.

I didn't know when or how but, I knew it was on the horizon. This particular afternoon I felt my heavenly language stirring up on the inside of me and I began speaking in tongues fluently with endless streams of tears.

In that moment I knew God still loved me and hadn't left me nor forsaken me.

He was waiting on me to humble myself and return to him, he never left me I walked away and abandoned my relationship with him.

Let me pause right here, right now and give God a well deserving SHOUT of Praise!!! And rebuke every religious spirit that would try to put limits on the move and power of the living God.

GOD meant me right where I was left for dead, forgotten about, looked over and counted out not only by the church folk but, I had given up on my own self as well.

We serve a limitless God that is not intimidated by our sick sin symptoms and issues, who is long suffering and when you call on him he answers.

No matter where you are, I dare you to call on JESUS in spite of your wayward self HE never take a break from being the incredible God he alone is.

God is a way maker, miracle working, promise keeper, light in the darkness God that not only hear our prayers but faithful to answer them in his perfect timing.

Fast forward, November 2010 two weeks after my granddaughter Kai was born into the world God lead me out of that relationship and lifestyle supernaturally permanently from that day on.

Her birth to me was what Moses birth was to the children of Israel, Baby born for deliverance.

though, I was finally physically free I was still emotionally, mentally and spiritually in bondage. I became a slave to my job and worked so much overtime in fear of not having enough, so much so that I worked 7 days a week straight and a lot of times those days included working double shifts.

Total trust was my issue and biggest challenge so I went on trying to make it happen on my own, my way. God began to inform me that he was my Source and that my job was a resource. I was gradually getting to FAITH slowing but surely.

Proven Closure

I wanted to prove to myself, my family, friends and even the world, that I wasn't gay especially the x who I slipped back into bed with through the lame excuse and justification that we both used about never having closure, it's just another excuse to fulfill our flesh.

Truth be told we both had our own personal motives to prove one to the other that it could happen between us again.

There was one other guy I regrettably gave into after years of denying his advancements, whom I really began to like a lot after getting to know him a little better and fostering a closer friendship.

He seemed to be a legit person and genuine friend until his true colors were revealed and exposed in the worse way. These hard knocks were valuable lessons I had to learn and move pass in order to get me in position and closer to my breakthrough. when the smoke cleared I was still broken and in need of wholeness that only God could provide.

Back to plan A after a lifetime of exploring through plan B thru Z

I share these truths with great passion in hope to prevent someone else from falling into these pitfalls.

THERE IS A WAY THAT SEEMS RIGHT
TO MAN, BUT IT'S END IS THE WAY
TO DEATH.

PROVERBS 14:12

Manisfestation

C elibacy became my portion and the word of God became my meat and drink, shortly after I began fostering a friendship with a fellow employee on my job 12 years my senior. She invited me to attend church with her on June 5th 2016 a day that will go down in history in my life's journal it was on this date that I was truly converted and received my miracle.

During praise and worship the heavens opened and I was taken up into a realm of the spirit in which I had never experienced before, although I was in a mega church in a crowed sanctuary I had a one on one face to face encounter with the living God.

I don't know how to fully explain my encounter and experience but, I can assure you that God himself performed major spiritual surgery on me in that moment, he gave me a mind and heart transplant. Instantly I knew I was made new miraculously right then and there.

Yes! I am a sign, miracle and wonder in real time by a real GOD. if you don't believe me ask God or my children they all are credible sources who knows me best and personally.

God's anointing broke and destroyed that monetarist spirit of perpetual backsliding off my life that kept me bound for 32 years and a slave to instability and stagnation.

He literally reversed the curse of disobedience and turned my obedience into a blessed life. He changed my name from hopeless to HOPE DEALER and gave me the assignment to Deal Hope to the HOPELESS.

WHAT an Amazing and Incredible GOD we Serve.

After major spiritual surgery to place the healing process began, as God walked with me step by step he begin to fine tune my ear to hear his voice clearly and developed my obedience on demand as he conditioned my character through many test, trials, purging, pruning, cutting, molding, breaking, stretching while stripping off me the residue of the world.

Just when I thought it was a completion of my conditioning He said daughter now you are ready for boot camp.

I was looking at God like are you trying to kill me? and He made it crystal clear that's exactly what he was doing and was going to cut my head off too to assure my old nature didn't resurrect again, because we are our own worse enemy. I said MY GOD what do you call all that I just went through? He said THAT was the warm up session you are just getting started he then instructed me to shut my self in my own house.

He informed me that he was my shepherd and that he was placing me in spiritual critical care and he couldn't trust me in the hands of common man in this season of my life.

He said I have restored, confirmed, and strengthen you and will establish you myself I am your Source and will provide all your needs.

The water of the word washed me from the inside out so much so I didn't recognize myself and for a while in sheer amazement how God had changed my desires and passions completely.

His refiner's fire kept me on course and layers upon layers began to fall and loose me daily.

The more I emptied myself the more he poured into me with great love, grace, compassion and tender mercies.

Today I have identified my identity in the relentless LOVE of God through his son Jesus Christ. Today, I'm whole, delivered and set free by becoming one with the one who created me.

Today, I know my assignment, calling and purpose in the kingdom of God here on the earth. I walk in integrity by the grace of God by his holy spirit in Power, Dominion and Authority.

I influence others by example as I'm lead by demonstration through the supernatural flow of God's presence in every area of my life.

When I passed by you again and saw you behold, you were at the age for LOVE and I spread the corner of my garment over you and covered your nakedness I made a vow to you and entered into covenant with you declares the Lord God, and you became mine. Ezekiel 6:8

17

The infinite wisdom of God blows my mind, remember my journey began with my parents being 17years of age at the time of my birth and then at 17 I was plagued with that generational curse along my own personal journey and then again at 17 I was violated and fondled by a very close family member during a out of town family reunion trip.

Well God in his infinite wisdom used the very thing that tried to keep itself attached to me in a negative aspect and bound by defeat to announce my Victory in him in FULL CIRCLE.

Let me help you understand a little further during my cave season my dear sister friend prophetess Michelle Smith introduced me to Ambassador Sophia Ruffin's Ministry through a video she in boxed to my phone.

In the beginning of 2017, follow me... immediately I knew this was a divine connection ordained by God after I fully viewed the message. I began following her ministry on social media from that day forward.

Sophia's T.V. feed me like the ravens feed Elijah in my cave season.

I wasn't able to attend the CBK Conference 2k17 but I ordered the live stream and immediately after she announced open registration for 300 CBK SQUAD I registered asap because I knew this was a door GOD had provided for me to enter through.

On Wednesday September 27, 2017 I received a message from Sophia Ruffin that stated I was drafted for the Come Back Kid Squad and when I received my winning Jersey number no other than 17 the wisest man on earth couldn't set that up no way, no how and I had never personally meant SOPHIA at that time.

No man on earth could be that strategic outside of God, He's like No other and no one can compare to our Great God.

HE'S INCREDIBLE ALL BY HIMSELF!!!

For I know the plans I have for you, declares the LORD, plans of peace and not evil, to give you a future and a hope.

Jeremiah 29:11

Daughter of Destiny

The journey continues with you using the gifts God has invested on the inside of you in conjunction with the tools this section of the book will provide for you.

No matter where you are in your journey God will meet you at your starting point willing and ready to walk you through your personal deliverance every step of the way he never leaves nor forsake us.

It wasn't easy telling my story for the world to see but, it was important for me to share my story in order to stir up the story in you.

We overcome the enemy by the blood of the lamb and the word of our testimony.

Pay and Pray Forward, Faith Without Works are dead.

it's imperative for your journey of inner healing to begin now, the fact that you have this book in your hand is a sign that the process has begun for your personal walk towards WHOLENESS.

God want you completely healed totally evolved from emotional trauma and set free in the matchless name of Jesus who died in our place for that very purpose.

It's high time to be emptied of all the toxins and poisonous memories that has constantly robbed us of a healthy and victorious lifestyle of the overflow of God's living water.

Are you ready to win on the winning team?

Do you know what your earthy assignment consist of?

You were born with purpose daughter of destiny and I believe you can do all things through Christ who strengthens you.

I may or may not know you personally but, one thing I'm certain of is the fact that God had you in mind when he gave me this assignment and there is no one who knows you better than he does and he knows exactly what you need when you need it.

I love you and hope my story has helped you realize that JESUS is the only way, truth and the life unto God the Father who is alive and wants to operate his will through the plans he has for your life.

For you formed my inward parts, you knitted me together in my mother's womb, I will praise you, for I am fearfully and wonderfully made.

Psalm 139: 13,14

Journaling Your Journey

U TILIZE this section of the book as a tool to Schedule yourself time and space to put in the necessary work that will put you in the right posture and position for your mega shift and breakthrough.

Pour out every feeling and thought that make you sick on the inside. No more suppressing or bottling up your true feelings you have permission from your heavenly father to Release, Release, Release in Jesus name It is your season to Evolve From Emotional Trauma.

LET'S GO!!!!! I WILL MEET YOU ALL ON THE OTHER SIDE of expressing yourself in your own unique way, Ready Set and Go!!!

THINGS I'D LOVE FOR YOU TO KNOW THAT I NEVER SHARED WITH YOU...

MY THOUGHTS OF THE MILESTONES YOU MISSED IN MY LIFE THAT I WANTED TO SHARE ESPECIALLY WITH YOU...

TIMES I WATCHED OTHERS BOND WITH THEIR MOM WHEN YOU WERE MIA...

THESE ARE THE VISIONS I HAD OF OUR CONNECTION...

THE THINGS I REMEMBER MOST ABOUT YOU...

DEAR MOMMA,

DEAR MOMMA

JOURNALING MY JOURNEY HELPS ME TO REALIZE I DESERVE TO BE HEARD AND MY FEELINGS MATTER...

SHOUT OUT TO...

SHORTCUT TO.

HERE'S MY TRIBUTE...

THE GREAT GIFT I FOUND IN A GRANDMOTHER I LONGED FOR IN A MOTHER...

IF I HAD THE CHANCE TO TELL MY TRUE STORY I WOULD BEGIN WITH SAYING...

MOM YOU WERE IRREPLACEABLE EVEN IN YOUR ABSENCE...

YOUR CHOICES CONCERNING ME IMPACTED EVERY ASPECT OF MY LIFE...

THESE WERE MY MOST AWKWARD MOMENTS...

MY UNSAID EXPERIENCES HURTED ME THE MOST ...

I LIVED IN A BUBBLE OF FEAR IMPARTED BY YOUR REJECTION AND ABANDONMENT...

SHYNESS COVERED UP MY SHAME AND SELF HATE...

YOUR MAUDLIN MOMMY MOMENTS LEFT ME PERPLEXED WITH MIXED EMOTIONS...

MISSING YOU PUT ME IN MELODRAMATIC MODE...

I LONGED TO GET THE CHANCE TO COMMUNICATE WITH YOU ONE ON ONE...

ARTICULATING MY TRUE HEART IS MY NEW ART...

You Made It!!!

BELOVED, I promised you that I would meet you on the other side and I would like to be the first one to CONGRATULATE you for putting forth the effort and doing the work to make a intentional difference in your own life by taking the necessary initial steps that will jumpstart your journey towards freedom from emotional trauma thumbs up for you!!! Keep Going Forth and never STOP.

Welcome to the next step of your journey of deliverance that leads you to your destiny as you continue on the path of Evolving from emotional trauma.

Therefore, if anyone is in Christ he is a new creation the old has passed away, behold the new has come.

2Corinthians 5:17

My personal shares...
Here are a few inserts from my personal healing journal.

As far back as I could remember I always wished and prayed that my mom could be everything I needed her to be for me as her daughter.

I wanted my mom to love me to life and adore me with her eyes.

I needed my mom's advice and undivided attention.

I wished for one on one time with my mom throughout my upbringing.

I longed for my mom to nurture and care for me when I was sick or didn't feel well.

I wanted my mom to tell me her childhood stories.

I day dreamed about my mom taking me shopping for pretty things that would make me feel pretty.

I wanted my mom to sing to me and read bedtime stories to me before tucking me in at night.

I needed my mom's nurturing, love, hugs and kisses a bond I never experienced with my biological mom.

For my father and mother have forsaken me, but the LORD will take me in.

Psalm 27:10

Delia Adams, serving founder of Replenish ministries and ambassador for Christ who promotes victorious living in the overflow of God's daily presence and relentless love in every area of your life. Delia resides in Philadelphia, Pennsylvania mother of two adult daughters Brandy and Briana one granddaughter Kai and one grandson Idris.

Delia the Hope Dealer

is available for speaking events and
book signings upon request
Email: **deliaadams5@gmail.com**
Follow on Facebook: Delia Adams
Join me and share my REPLENISH A.P.B.
(Anointed People Back To God) Exhortations
and Periscope Delia Adams @Replenish

Prayer Of Salvation

Heavenly Father, I believe that Jesus Christ is your son, and that he died on the cross to save me from my sin. I believe that he rose again to life, and that he invites me to live forever with him in heaven as a part of your family. Because of what Jesus has done, I ask you to forgive me of my sin and give me eternal life. I invite you to come into my heart and life. I want to trust Jesus as my savior and follow him as my lord. Help me to live in a way that pleases and honors you. Amen!!!!

Because, if you confess with your mouth that Jesus is Lord and believe in your heart that God raised him from the dead, you will be saved. Romans 10:9

If you have accepted God's Gift of salvation by his amazing grace through his only begotten son JESUS please share your great news so that I can celebrate with you to the Glory of God for your Victory!!!!!

I would love to formally welcome you either into or back to the family of GOD and make sure you are in a good place that will encourage your spiritual growth and maturity.

I Love you but, GOD himself LOVES YOU BEST Today, Tomorrow and forevermore.